Broken Like Shattered Glass

Living in the Past

by

Simone

Broken Like Shattered Glass: Living in the Past

Author: Simone

Copyright © Simone (2025)

The right of Simone to be identified as author of this work has been asserted by the author in accordance with section 77 and 78 of the Copyright, Designs and Patents Act 1988.

First Published in 2025

ISBN 978-1-83538-884-6 (Paperback)
978-1-83538-885-3 (E-Book)

Book cover design and Book layout by:
 White Magic Studios
 www.whitemagicstudios.co.uk

Published by:
 Maple Publishers
 Fairbourne Drive, Atterbury,
 Milton Keynes,
 MK10 9RG, UK
 www.maplepublishers.com

The views expressed in this work are solely those of the author and do not reflect the opinions of Publishers, and the Publisher hereby disclaims any responsibility for them. This book should not be used as a substitute for the advice of a competent authority, admitted or authorized to advise on the subjects covered.

A CIP catalogue record for this title is available from the British Library.

All rights reserved. No part of this book may be reproduced or translated by any form or by any means, electronic or mechanical, including photocopying, recording or by any information storage and retrieval system without written permission from the author.

CONTENTS

- Those Eyes..................4
- G..................5
- You..................7
- Seasonal Baby..................8
- A New Lesson..................9
- Sleeping Sweetly..................10
- Better..................11
- She's like the wind..................12
- Him..................13
- Headache..................14
- SNM..................16
- Every Girl..................17
- La Luna..................19
- What is fair?..................20
- Rhythm..................21
- The Battle..................22
- Them..................23
- Never..................25
- All of Us..................26
- How long..................27
- Mr..................33
- Dawn..................34
- Friends..................35
- Looking Out..................36
- Know Your Worth..................37
- Hiding..................39
- Riddle..................40
- Onelia..................41
- Where do you go?..................42
- The Game..................43
- Issues!..................44
- Sitting in the moonlight!..................46

- Future 47
- What's next? 48
- Regret! 49
- Softly 50
- You Should Know Better! 51
- Four Letters 53
- Untitled 55
- Be Careful 57
- Eyes 58
- Convenient ey! 59
- Dreaming! 60
- Whom 61
- Find Me! 62
- To: Me, From: Me 63
- Up Against the Wind! 66
- Looking Glass 68
- Silence! 69
- K 70
- All In My Mind 72
- Written 74
- Distracted 75
- Memories Back Then 76
- Disguised 78
- Like Shattered Glass 79

Those Eyes

In everyone's eyes tells a story, tells a story that bounds in the depth of your soul.

In my eyes there's a story, a story that reads you.
So, I'm not going to tell you you're amazing,
I'm not going to tell you how you make me smile,
I'm not going to say you're always on cue
I won't tell you you're a beautiful sensation.
I refuse to mention how you keep me warm
and you are there even when I don't need you.

I won't tell you because I want you to read the story my heart spells and my soul tells.
I won't mention my satisfaction.
I'm not keeping secrets; I'm not telling you lies,
I just want you to look into my eyes and you can tell me what they say.
Do they speak of beautiful innocence?

I've looked into the eyes of many but only yours tell the story, somewhat similar to mine. It shows connection, it reminds me of a story I read daily when I look in the mirror.

There are always two sides to one story.
I proved that the day when I first looked into your eyes and they told me you're the other part of my story.

G

I want to know you for you, I don't want to keep guessing.
I want you to talk to me, let me in, don't just expect me to know things.
Just like I want you to look at me for me, don't judge me, ask me.
Let's have a conversation, not a guessing game.

I don't want to play games.
I want to be serious and be for real, not pretend.
I won't do soon or eventually; I want to do right now.
I want to be able to look in your eyes and smile because I understand and know, not look in your eyes and smile because I'm really laughing to myself in confusion.

I want you for you, for that smile, those lips, that brain and those thoughts, for those eyes and soul full of charisma.
I want to smile because you made me smile.
I want to tingle when you touch me and when you hug me, to not want to let go.
I want you to hold me until forever not until tomorrow.
I want you here today and tomorrow not now and whenever.

Smile................because I'm smiling back.

Remember this, don't remember me.
I don't want you to remember me, I want you to have me and miss me.

I want when I cry, it's because we've come to learn a new lesson in life together not because you made me cry.

I want to take that journey I've thought of.
I want to take this journey, I want to take this path, this here and now with you.

You

You are my life
You are my light
You are the reason I cry at night.
You make me smile
You make me laugh
But sometimes you tell me lies.

I feel vulnerable, I feel unworthy but yet I still want more of you.
I'm never satisfied by the little pieces you give me.
I always want more, yes, I'm a bit greedy but I can't help it if you are Just so..........

I tell myself I've had enough.
I'll tell myself to stop
I'll lie and lie and lie again just to comfort my heart.
But NO MORE, no pretending, no more trying.

I told myself yesterday that I'll just move on and have fun.
Have no relationships, no more paranoia just to take it day by day but tomorrow I'll think of you and want to try again.

If I start this with no strings attached, it'll be dangerous because the strings will start to grow, then you'll just take the scissors and cut them off. Then I'll be falling way down into oblivion where no one can help but you, but you'll be gone like the wind and stolen the rest of my heart.

Seasonal Baby

As I watch the snow, it's so beautiful as it lives in the sky and dies on the floor.
So amazing as it falls to touch the many lives in this mysterious place we call life, no answers as to why it all occurs.

When rain falls it seems to remind me of all the bad that's happened, then it all gets washed away.
Drop by drop, splash on splash, puddle by puddle, stream down stream, washing it away bit by bit, day by day but as each day dawns more sorrow rises, like it rained for no reason.

When the summery sun comes out, the glow sets on my face creating a never-ending smile, the warmth like the love of someone holding you telling you, you are safe and its ok.

The fresh spring breeze as it blows through my hair as if it were clearing my mind of all negativities, leaving the pure.

To stand and gaze as each leaf fall slowly gliding to the floor to join the rest gathered, to feel as though it belonged, be a part of it all.
Makes you wonder if that's the journey we take, just in a more creative manner

A New Lesson

As a child we are told "play with fire and you'll get burned". When what they should have told us was "don't play with fire if you can't control it".

It's all happening around me and I have no control; I don't even think I know how to take control.

Sitting clueless about the world, thinking I've seen and heard it all but as each day dawns a new experience, acknowledgement, understanding it all will take a while.
Accepting it all will take more than time and patience.

I sit looking out on the world trying to understand what's happening and why they happen yet still no conclusion.
So, I stop for a moment to realise, I'm trying to read the forbidden book of life.

I look at you in fascination and curiosity, trying to find ways to understand your mind and ways of thinking.
All this just to get from phase one to phase two, to from being friend to future.
I don't understand the sudden interest or why it won't go away but I need to quench my heart's thirst for you.

Sleeping Sweetly

Sleeping sweetly in his warm and tender arms.

A smile on her face that glowed in the dark, lighting the room.
Filled with such an amazing feeling, it blocked all other possible thought.
She held on tightly, never wanting to let go as she slipped off to dream.

A priceless moment to keep.

The morning came, as she opened her eyes to lie there to watch his innocence.
His eyes opened slowly with a reassuring smile and a kiss gently placed on her forehead.

This moment in every life is of that sublime joy, that makes all things seem possible, forgiving the past, letting go the regret, proceeding into tomorrows unforeseen.

Better

I feel better in the day, I feel stronger, but it's when I'm all alone with my thoughts at night, when there's nothing else to think of but you.

Tears start to roll down my face onto my pillow and that won't stop till slumber.

It gets better and easier each day, but the nights seem to take more time, because I think of whence, I was wrapped up in your arms where nothing could hurt me but then that became you and that hurt the most.

2010 hurt the most, caused a lot of issues and pain.

It helped me to forget 2009 and 2008.

Made me better but it hurt the most, but I've learned, and I've grown, for 2011 is the beginning of a new me.

Change what I once could not, the happier me, go forth and embrace it all with a risk and a chance to dare.

Hello Me!

She's like the wind

Like the waves that washed away my footprints or the snow that covered my tracks, the wind shall blow me out of your life but unlike the waves and snow I will leave a mark behind.
A mark of regret where you wish you hadn't lost me.

The hurt I once suffered, I've now recovered.
I won't blame you because what hurt the most was the belief I kept up that you could never cause me this pain.

I took a picture of my future and came back only to show you I'll be doing just fine without you.
You may be here today but gone tomorrow, happy to have met you, glad to have lost you and I say this with a smile.

None better, some worse
Truth is there all the same.
They're capable of loving and caring but their natural instinct causes pain.
Pain only a woman can bear, live through and survive.

I'm still here and living strong.

Him

He stole my heart
Refuses to give it back
but doesn't need it.
                He makes me smile with out trying
                but causes hurt in the same.
Each day, it's torn more
a pain I can't bear but
yet I stick around.
                You think he cares in what he says
                but proves other wise in what he does.

I want to know.
but to hear the truth for myself makes me wish I hadn't asked.
I see the hurt you are capable of, but I cannot seem to leave.
Each day new tears caused by an old source.
I want to move on, but I'm stuck.

You can't change people, so don't live in the dream where you think you can.
"The truth hurts"

"You can't handle the truth"

"Is honesty the best policy?"
You tell me a lie; I dig for the truth.
You tell the truth, it causes pain.
You came with a warning; I chose to ignore.
Now I suffer with the consequences of falling hard.

Headache

Understanding you, would be like trying to draw blood from stone.

With you around, makes me feel like I'm on a never-ending carousel, forever feeling dizzy, not sure if my feet are on the floor or floating.
When my feet finally touch the floor, I feel like I'm walking on eggshells always having to tip toe around, to not make a sound or cause upset.

Feels like I'm aiming to please you and have forgotten about myself, drawn into your amazing charm, blinded by it; only fooling myself to ignore the arrogant, inconsiderate, selfish reality you are.

Everything to please you, not to upset you, keep you happy; all I hear is "you, you, you".
Yes, you include me, yes your plans include me, yes you do nice things for me, the only time you are calm and not as selfish is, if I'm sick.

Round and round I go, my thoughts going at 100mph.
Soon I shall fall to the floor, when there's nothing to hold onto or keep me up.
Then I shall wait for the room to stop spinning; then stand my ground to walk away from the carousel.

Proven – everything that's shiny, pretty or seems like fun is NOT always a good idea.

They say lightning doesn't strike in the same place twice. Maybe I'm thinking this is my lightning and can't let go, BUT better must come.

No longer you, you, you – lets try me, me, me.

SNM

Say no more! There's nothing more to say!
There's no more you can say now! I've heard it all.
the chat up lines, the sweet lies
the sex talk, the let down excuses.
I've seen the 'I want you' look to the 'I love you' look to the 'I'm about to break your heart look.'

I'm tired of the senseless but heart melting make-up songs.
I don't want anymore reasons to forgive a selfish tortured soul.
They're all valid reasons, yes, they make sense BUT I'm at breaking point, a point of no return, the point where nothing is an acceptable excuse to forgive you just that once more.

Just stop! Yes you did wrong, yes I'm still naive enough to forgive you but guess what? I'm just not that stupid to take you back for the thousandth time!

It took me a while.
I'm soft hearted and forgiving but even the fool knew when to hit the punch line.

So yes, I forgive you, no I don't hate you
Yes you did me wrong, no you haven't learned your lesson.

Soo Say No More!

Every Girl

Every girl wants a guy who knows all their flaws, all the struggles that come with loving her and still think she's worth the trouble.

A relationship is a very complex thing and there are many different forms.
It's all just not as simple as 1, 2, 3 anymore.

So you have to sit and think to yourself, is it all worth the trouble and heartache.
Questions many elders have struggled to answer through out the generations.

I sit and wonder about my own complex, complicated relationship.
Flaws at each end, tears at every turn, argument in every sentence and yet a make-up and forgive all at each dawn.
Days where I want to say, "forget it all" and days where I would fight the good fight, keep my calm, just to keep it together and keep it in my life.
Losing it might be more painful than the daily struggle.

Today is a silent day but a loud thought, shouting at myself, debating fewer pros than cons, but they just seem the worth.
Where one pro knocks out ten cons, one pro justifies five cons.
Saying it out loud makes you seem that much crazier.

Two stubborn souls cannot live, which makes being the bigger person make me feel ever so small at times.

To back down when you know you are right seems foolish but to back down on the terms of love all makes sense.

What's in the dark must come to light and just because you can see straight through to the other side doesn't mean when you get there, that it's still as foreseen.

What hurts the most is when you want them more than they want you, when they don't see you and know how much you would do for them, when they take advantage because you care.

A girl can only dream of that one sweet day soon.

La Luna

You can't outshine me
You can't outrun me
You can't hide from me.
I'm always here for you, especially at night
I will never abandon you
Whenever you're feeling alone, just look to the sky.

With the stillness of the night and the silence in the clouds
A warm breeze and a comforting thought,
A smile upon my face but a tear drop in my eye.

Reflected in the water, as the waves washed up on my feet.
The moment is seized and a moment of laughter.
An indescribable aroma came with a pleasant feeling.
Sometimes I sit to wonder- is it all real?

You're here, I can see you, I can feel you but is it true thus I can't reach out and touch you.

What is fair?

It's not fair to take what is not yours,
But is it fair to see what you want and not get it.

Simple actions cause big events
A little secret may cause havoc
What is hidden in the dark will soon come to light.

I came with pure intentions
Corruption came along, I fought for as long as I could,
Eventually gave into temptation but brought no satisfaction.

The joy I expected found a pain unforeseen.

No physical pain can never compare to heartache.

Rhythm

The beat in my heart matches the rhythm in my soul.

To enjoy my life each day as it comes, living and breathing my happiness.

Worry not about tomorrow, for fears of tomorrow will only spoil today.

Don't analyze your choices. Take risks, live in the moment, good or bad there's always another day to make change.

The Battle

How many times must I go through this with myself?
It's like my mind, heart and soul are in a never-ending battle.

My mind makes perfect sense, but my heart matches a good argument and then my soul is stuck in the middle being unheard and ignored.
My mind says "go", my heart argues its case to stay, and my soul ever so confused.
Lost my focus, strayed too far.

Nao consigo deixar-te ir, preciso-te aqui comigo ....
(I can't let you go; I need you here.....)

Beautiful smile caught my attention from across the way.
Loved him from the day I said his name aloud.

Fighting for a love that isn't truly yours is a big challenge, fighting to win it over is the adventure.

I don't want to hurt but I chose to stay, I want to be happy, but I chose to suffer.

Them

They are nice, they show interest.
They seem keen, they play it safe.
They treat you, they show you they are capable of love and care for you.
They keep you company, keep you warm.
They make you feel that feeling we need to feel.
They make us feel good, but they are just stringing us along.
They keep us on our toes, they keep us happy.
They convince us that they are 'the one'.

They chase us until they get us to chase them and then they stop.
Everything just STOPS!

They maybe grown but will always be little boys, who play with their toys and when they get bored they put them back in the toy chest.
That's what they do, they treat us like toys.
All fun when it's new and shiny and interesting; but then they get bored and lose interest until a new toy comes along.
This is where they miss out, where they go wrong.

We stick around through the good, great and amazing, down till they turn sour to the selfish, manipulating, stubborn, inconsiderate, and ungrateful that they are underneath.
Yet they don't think they've done any injustice.

They throw away the valuable toys that have been there from day one but keep the new cheap, shiny soon to tarnish plastic that won't be able to stand up to the weather.
Only then they will remember the good ones.

We should look at them how they look at us.
When they come they are shiny, amazing and wonderful.
Soon as they start to tarnish and become selfish; we should throw them out and don't look back.

No such thing as a perfect and almost doesn't count.
Stop thinking you are not good enough or that we have to live up to their perfection because it's all just a hallucination.

Simone

Never

Never judge a book by its covers.
Every page, every chapter reveals another piece.
Another piece of why the book is what it is.

On the outside could be old, worn and disfigured but on the inside reveals an amazing beauty beyond your imagination.
Every chapter better than it's last.

The cover of the book is only the way you see it,
Because of how you treat it.
So next time treat it with better care.

A young girl with an older guy, eventually she will start to seem older be it from maturity or just plain stress of the relationship.

All of Us

We all do bad things, make bad choices, do things we said we would never do again.

We're bound to make mistakes along the way, and we're entitled to them, they help us to learn but who are you to criticise and look down on me?
If I didn't make those mistakes, I wouldn't be the person I am now, and you wouldn't be you either.

Yes, you're entitled to voice your opinions so I may not fall into life's same trap of bad choices and horrendous outcomes but if we don't learn the lessons ourselves, we won't truly learn.

We have a habit of doing what we're told not to do.
I don't call it disobedience, I call it wanting to live life and experience everything, even the forbidden.
Taking a chance, playing in the rain even when you know you are not supposed to.
If we don't. How will we know what rain feels like and why we shouldn't do it because we'll catch a cold?

One is the shell and the other the alter ego!
Try everything, fear nothing.

How long

How long does it take a broken heart to heal, a tortured soul to be at peace, an unstable mind to calm and puffy, cried out, swollen eyes to rejuvenate?

I've stayed up too many nights crying, wishing, praying and dreaming for something to change, thus only fooling myself to believe it was possible.
Wanted it soo bad, wanted it to be real, it eventually clouded my judgement.

Not in the right mind to make drastic decisions but I did.
Doing irrational things, forgiving hurtful things against my better normal judgement, things I wouldn't, couldn't and shouldn't forgive, I did.
Blinded! This thing called love.

Took me a long time to admit to myself that's what it was, my biggest hurt was I was in love with the idea of love and not the reality that he could never love me back the way I needed to.

Fell into a spiral of wallow, depression but sticking a smile on.
Lived in denial so long, pretending it didn't hurt, that I didn't care, that I was ok.
Dying on the inside, my mind slowly deteriorating, my heart beating at abnormal pace, living with this pain I can't describe a pain no woman should suffer.

Building up my strength daily, building belief I'm over the past, weeks go by and I'm on top of the world.

With the thought of moving on in my mind, a smile on my face, then in an instant you pop back up and I crumble and fall right back where I was.

Wanting you, fighting myself to stay away, but I'm weak.

Ending up right where I didn't want to be AGAIN.
Music in the background trying to drown out my thoughts, but my heart is in so much pain, screaming out over the music, always to be heard.

Eventually I block it out, ignoring it, feeling better for a while.

Beginning the moving on process, I'm getting there, THEN ONCE AGAIN he comes back making me second guess all my future options.
Am I doing it to get over the past or running or just using it as an excuse to just seem happy?

I want to move on, l want to get away from the past, to be happy but it's hard, I fell really hard for a soul who couldn't return the favour, which made the pain more severe.
I ask myself once again "How long does it take a broken heart to heal, a tortured soul to be at peace, an unstable mind to calm and puffy, cried out, swollen eyes to rejuvenate?"

I really need some help. I can't do it on my own but my pride refuses to burden another soul with my complaints though talking to myself just makes me that much crazier each day.

On my way forward but something keeps pulling me back, its time to stop.
If I can't get what I need from the past, I need to find a new future, something that's right for me.

Someone once said, "it's easy to find someone who can **** you like no other but it's hard to find someone who can truly love you like no other".

Funny how we find saying that relate to our lives, it gives a comfort that someone else out there can relate to me.

I found the one who could **** me like no other but still waiting to find the guy who can love you like no other.

This is where I went wrong, I was waiting for him to love me like no other when deep down I knew he wouldn't.

What hurt the most was knowing he actually could but chose not to.

The thing that could break a woman, knowing they are capable of loving you but choose not to.

We drive ourselves crazy, questioning ourselves if "there's just something about me" losing self confidence.

Men/women should stop trying to change women/men it never works like that.

A friend of mine said "the man/woman should want to change for themselves for the woman/man".

Foolish enough we still try for whatever reason.

I fell in love with the idea of love and what it would be like with him, how good it all seemed, obsessed with an idea that blinded me, to ignore all the disrespectful deceits, the heartache; I chose to close my eyes because the idea was better than the reality.

I can't stand feeling like this, a constant heartache, feeling stupid causing myself grief, punishing myself where I don't deserve it.
Why fight for a lost cause, no matter how bad you may want it.
If its just going to cause you pain, let it go!
Each day gives me a reason to want it, by night fall I'm miserable all over again.
All I ask for is happiness and all I get is pain.

"We ignore the one who love us, adore the ones who ignore us, love the ones who hurt us and hurt the ones who love us."
Why is love so blind to the truth?
Past!
Let the past stay in the past, don't let it haunt you with its beautiful memories of back when, thus always hiding the tears and pain caused by who you never thought could.
Remembering how foolish you were is the only chance you have to not make the same mistake again.

Tomorrow is unknown but sure as hell better than yesterday no matter how gloomy.
Just one more step no matter how small, just one leading to that something better.

Dreaming is me being persistent to get what I need to make it reality.
Head held high, walking on air never to look down or behind to ensure I don't fall back to that place I don't deserve to be.

Trying to think positive but you are bound to try break me.

You're a hazard for me, dangerous territory to tread on, always seeming to be just what I need, the further I tread to realise its not all warm goodness but a fire burning.

A lie to get where you needed, even the ones who knew better than to listen or fall for the bullshit, eventually sometimes slip up.

Keep an open mind but low expectations, minimal chance of disappointment and heartache.
I'm leaving for the last time, tired of turning back with the slightest hope of chance, only to be hit in the face with cruel reality.
No more looking back, if I left it behind, there's a reason I walked away from it.
Never take your past with you, you're destined to fall.
It holds you back, forget the wrong they did to you, forgive the pain they caused, let it all go and leave the past where it lies.
Only take with you, that hard lesson you learnt, take heed "what not to do".

Forget all about those heart felt songs you listened to, cried your eyes out to with that empty space on the bed.

Mr

Just because you can't see "Mr Better" anywhere in sight, doesn't mean he's not coming.

Don't look for "Mr Right" because it was just yesterday you thought "Mr Gorgeous" was him, but he turned out to be "Mr Selfish" and made you "Mrs Heartbroken".

Better will come into your life and you'll forget about the past hurt and just smile.
Though time may seem to be your foe, make patience your best friend; then happiness will be your reality.

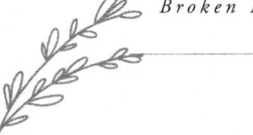

Dawn

City outside my window.......

As the sun goes down, I stand looking out onto its horizon, like nothing I've ever seen.
How the sun reflects off the clouds and onto the glass and warmth on my face, a smile as the light brightens the brown in my eyes, glistening as nature takes course.

The time of day that's filled with pure beauty as you watch the changes take place ever so quickly, colours change as do each moment.

Bright in the sky, slowly goes down to shine light on the other side.
Changing of colours change to darkness, only 'then' do the city lights shine.
As I stand high above looking down onto the night life.

Friends

As I get older, I realise our friendship was just based on a childhood dream.
Now you're older I realise what kind of friend you are!
One that I don't need but one that I will truly miss.

I pause to take a look at the people in my life; some I hold so dear and some who inspire me to just walk away and start fresh.

As time goes by, people change with various reasons, whether it be money or they just grew out of their old self.
The people we love may hurt us or they might leave, its not to say they never cared, they've just outgrew that person we once thought we knew. What it does tend to show is their true colours, the person they were destined to be and the person that was just being covered up.
Sad sometimes to lose that person you thought would always be there, there for you be it mentally, emotionally or physically.
Think carefully before you use the term 'best friend' because everything in life is momentary, nothing lasts 'forever' but cherish what you have while you have it or lose it faster than you ever thought.

I've lost faith in the part-time job which was our friendship.
Seems it was only me trying to keep it.
Tired of holding up a fragile foundation.

Looking Out

Sat on the windowsill looking to the sky, as the moon light glows across the sky, with the ocean breeze that swept the night's air.

She felt a pain in her chest, an attempt to come down and in an instant broken like shattered glass, falling to pieces on the floor. Pieces scattered across the room as she watched in realisation that she was still whole, but her heart shattered.

An attempt made to put the pieces back together turned disastrous.
Tears rolling down the cheek of a distraught soul, looking down to the misshapen object that was her heart.

A bright light filled the room; she looked through the window to the sky but 'twas not the moon.
She smiled to see reflected in glass the figure that stood behind her willing to lend a hand.

That heart was mine and that hand was yours, when you helped me mend that which was broken.

Know Your Worth

The eyes that watched, as I slipped through the fingers like running water, broken on the floor like shattered glass.

She has everything you want but made of nothing of what you need.
Short changed and less of an insult to injury.
Dreaming of forever, destined for failure.

The wise man said, "if you stand for nothing, you fall for everything."

Your head is up high but you brain is down low.
You run before you walk, talk before you think and regret before you've lived.
Two people seemed right for each other, yet wrong in all ways.

More than what meets the eye, not your typical girl.
I come with but an instruction on my label: 'handle with care.'
Give to receive, treat me how I deserve to be treated and live to be treated like a king.

All I want is someone to love me, WHOLE!
Not a part-time lover, not a momentary love, sometimes some days but all the time.
It will be a matter of time.
Take the time to find me, take your time to love me.
Don't love me today and forget tomorrow, hold me today and always.

Sometimes it just hurts when you fall for someone who doesn't catch you.
Something you wouldn't want to experience twice.
So you hide away expecting 'him' to find you.

Hiding

Locked away, forever, to never see the light of day.
The pain you suffered, I can't bear to put you through again.

Safe within the dark, never to be fooled by the light's hope.
A cruel injustice but formed by a protective mind.
You were left ever so fragile from your last encounter with the light, left shattered on the cold floor.

Maybe someday you will be strong enough to come out but for now you're safe, hidden behind the four walls I've built, covered with a pitch-black glass roof. Who only the 'right one' will know how to break to get to you.

The silence is brutal but the music, filled with so many lies.
Self Rehabilitation is what you need now, to stay warm and block out the cold.

I feel you beating with a slow, abnormal rhythm in my chest, too weak to catch up.

Riddle

Riddle me this, riddle me that; riddle me, riddle me, riddle me back.
I no longer understand a word that you say, everything has lost meaning. Sorry is at the top of the list, a bunch of letters thrown together supposed to mean you admit your guilt and want forgiveness, which I now have none left. Forgiven this, forgiven that; forgiven, forgiven until I had a heart attack. My abnormal beat in my chest, lost all its rhythm that holds me up, so weak and on my knees waiting for the strength to get back up.

Actions speak LOUDER than words,
Your words mean nothing to me anymore, goes through one ear and out the next just as they are formed by a creative tongue and spoken through lying lips, sounds so sweet to the ear but bitter to the brain.

Your greed makes you think with your lower brain.

I'm just lying to myself again; just not to face the truth that hurts so badly. It's not healthy but I do it, ignoring the obvious, once blinded by the fantasy that I wanted to be real, now just left feeling so angry at myself.

I look out, watching as each drop makes a splash on my windowpane, so peaceful. The clouds as they group together shadowing the beautiful moon and twinkling stars. Shifts my mind a drift on a calm. I now find myself wondering if anything was ever truthful.

Onelia

Taking my time to heal, I'm doing this my way in my own time.

As I sit staring at the stars questioning the moon, for how long I will feel this way.

They all say it will get better with time, but time is what I thought I had, that there would be enough to last me with happiness.

Faking a smile to hold the questions filled with curiosity. I've said it all before, tired of repetition.

As the day ends, with the sun going down leaving me to face the moon once more. Reminding me of the now lonely moment I'm stuck in. I sleep to get away but now I dream of the silence filled with no response.

My time here seems empty and unused left without purpose. That day will come where I can say I'm ok and mean it, that day where I can face the moon with a smile. The day where the silence is suddenly changed by the music.

It may not be now or tomorrow or the day after but as God is my witness, he reassures me that the day will come soon.

Where do you go?

Where do you go!?
Where is it that you disappear to when you close your eyes?

Where do you go? Where is that place you think of when you're holding me, looking into my eyes but staring at the depths of my soul?

Where do you go when the lights go out, when the air is warm, yet the temperature still rises? When my fingers run slowly down your back and my legs wrapped firmly around your waist.

Where does your mind travel to, the moment you're inside, the fever taking over your body,

Where is it that you go when the conversation stops, the loss of control of your upper mind and there›s nothing but feeling?

The Game

I won't fake a smile for a person only pretending to care. I won't try and be the bigger person if you're only going to belittle me. Treat me like a joke and I'll leave you like its funny.

I play to win; I leave my heart at home when I go out. I'm a better batsman than fielder so don't fall expecting me to catch you.

Hollow eyes, dark in the depths. Don't try to understand, accept it or walk away. Warm bodied and cold blooded. Don't let your eyes fool you. I'm the best at what I do, don't play with out reading the rule book.

Got tired of trying, I didn't give up I just stopped caring. He taught me one of life's most valuable lessons.

Not completely dead on the inside, just left my heart reserved in a box on the shelf.

Had a moment of weakness and nearly slipped up. They come in various varieties but not so different from one another. Careful, what you look for and what you see can be very different. So, stand for something or fall for anything.

Issues!

Issues! So many that I have.
Trying to catch up with my emotions is like a dog trying to catch its tail.

Unstable and unsure, what shall I do? I ask myself so many a time.

The heat, the passion, the tension and the sexual frustration. Why I do this to me is beyond reasonable understanding.

Heart and head constantly at war, no compromise and refuse to come to an agreement.

I grow tiresome and weary of it all. My body screams for him, my heart says go for it and my mind says lets keep it a secret. My eyes watching, my legs moving, my arms holding on, my heart racing and my mind blank.

My issues start with my head and end with my heart. Never in agreement, always leaving me unsure and won't take the risk and make a decision. I can't live in the moment until they're at peace.

What am I doing, why can't I just go for it, why do I care what others think or say, why do they need to know, no they don't need to know. Secrets always have a funny way of finding themselves to come to light, but I guess it's just better to leave it that way, a secret!

I will do just that, just that I'll do. secrets! Silent and deadly but harmless in the right minds, sealed mouths and crossed legs.

One, two, three maybe four but no one, not one, none the wiser.

Secrets are meant to be kept, I'm taking it to the grave, denying it to your life.

I have a secret, a secret that I'm taking to the grave. It's silent but deadly, it shall not come to the light. I won't tell you, no not even you.

Dreaming is reality because I am really dreaming. They came from my sub conscious, from past events, current events, déjà vu, and premonition of the feature. The crazy fun and wild shall come to pass. The secret I will never tell was a dream I had never foretell. My conscience is clear as glass because only I can see through it. What you don't know can't hurt you, so what they don't know can't haunt me.

Sitting in the moonlight!

With nothing but the open sky, the stars and moon light up the night as she sat so lonely on a torn lily pad.

She looked up to the sky hoping for an answer to the question playing in her mind.

Feet dipped in the shallow of the pond, testing the waters though it seemed cold.

Smiling as she looked at the lotus flower behind. A ray of hope in the thought: such beauty can come from the murkiest situation.

The broken watch at the bottom made it seem as though time itself had stopped. Her rippled reflection seemed broken with the night breeze.

For a split moment the night was silent and still not a cricket's chirp. The moon shone brighter, and a voice whispered, "it's ok to let go".

Future

What am I to do? Sit around waiting on a pipe dream? I look at my past and see where I went wrong, I change my present to mould my future. But anything worth it is ever easy to come by.

I've changed my path many a time and still got stuck and turned around. I sit to think what it is I want to do? Where is it I want to go? Where do I want to end up?

And there all in a fast minute I stopped and looked closely around. Kissing the floor saying, "what a beautiful escape."

As I walk on by, looking at the downfall of what I had hoped to gain in the past. All in shambles as I smile.

There's a reason behind everything that happens in life.

What's next?

Lost, washed up on shore, the waves washing up over me. The salt burning my eyes, feeling a bit sick of the vision I can't lose sight of. There's feeling in my legs, but I've lost the strength to get up and move. The burning sun beating down on me but still naive to not move. Its warmth was once a comfort vacation whereas now it's a burning hell I can't run from.

All emotions burnt out, leaving me unsure how and when to feel what. A wondering soul who came to rescue me, putting me in the shade but the confused ingrate I've become sees no gratitude but left with regret of being moved.

Who says moving on was an easy process?

A dark naive soul left to walk the path of denial. Trying to be comfortable in the new shade being able to look out at the light yet reminiscing about burning in the heat of the sun and blinded by the light she could see.

It's beautiful in the shade but afraid the sun will always get to me.

Regret!

Saddened by the sight she sees as she looks around the room, white walls everywhere. Her heart grieving for the place she calls home. Trapped with a broken heart caused by the bad choices she made, now facing the consequences. The one she cares the least for now is the one who cares most for her, teary eyed sun rise to sun set, praying daily to be set free from the suffering.

You cannot give a child their mind, you cannot make a mother love you if their heart is not for you, but you can always love them no matter what.

Softly

He spoke with a soft whisper, so fragile and barely heard. Staring deeply into my eyes as he looks through the window to my soul. A gentle caress as our lips meet, with the warm touch as he held me closely.

A moment so intimate in its own. As I laid my head on his chest, his heartbeat echoed. A pounding that seemed to sync with my own.

So comfortable, so peaceful and free, safe in his arms. The night was quiet, the air was warm. The moon light shone through and shimmered through the room. A captured moment, grasped for a short time.

The time spent together, so amazing. Made it harder when we were apart. To wake up with a smile daily. Knowing the pure love that made my heart sing.

I love being wrapped up in his rhythm and getting lost in the words he whispers, the sweet nothing's in my ear.

Music filling the air, the gentle breeze, his warm hands and hot body. Shivers running down my spine. My corrupt mind filled with temptation waiting to unfold.

Simone

You Should Know Better!

Selfish becomes you, couldn't care less about what happens to me. I'm not mad, I forgive you.

Deep down you are constantly fighting yourself, eating away at what once was a heart. Crying on the inside, angry on the outside, putting in a front of cold rough exterior but that's just not you.

We're more alike deep down than you pretend to be. You are bleeding and afraid to ask for help, but I can't help unless you let me.

I can't stick around guessing your pain. I'm afraid to grow and be happy, I'm afraid if I leave, you'll turn to ruins. I won't let myself be free, be happy, grow up and do me because I'll feel responsible for letting you get to yourself.

I can't live this way; I have to be sure you are going to be ok when I'm away.

What am I to do? **It›s just me and me in my head! Who looks after me when I look after the world. I take care of you and them but who takes care of me, there›s just not enough of me left to do the job. My energy is running low.**

What am I to do?

I sit alone looking up at the stars, talking to the moon, while all he does is smile down on me. The silence of the night so calm and still disturbed by the echoed fall of the first rain drop. Showering down, nothing sounds more bliss. Splashes down on my face washing my worries away.

Wondering what's to come!

Four Letters

It doesn't have to make sense, it's never logical. It's not physics nor math, it never adds up. It is what it is. It's not predictable and you never see it coming but when it happens you will definitely know.

We often get confused and unsure if it is when it does. Different colours and many shades. It never seems realistic, then you question your self. No matter how high or low, no matter the situation, it still is what it is.

Many hide behind the lies, many falsify it. You can't help the conclusion; it stays with you. We give and we share it.

Some don't believe in it, some have never found it. Some have tarnished it, and some are afraid of it. Some warn others away from it and put bad meaning behind it. Some have lost it and don't know how to try again but no one is immune from it. Written, it may seem little, or it may seem small but it's sound and reality have a huge effect on us.

Four letters that most men fear to utter. Four letters to be embraced, four letters to make it worth while.

Trust in it and it will have faith in you. Four letters to beat all odds, to keep you smiling. Those four letters, a gentle whisper to the ear, a lifetime of warmth to the heart.

Still dreaming of the one day soon to hear my four letters. The story behind it, the path that led to it. Battles I've had to win, wars I had to lose and the time I spent waiting.

Hope is still alive; faith keeps me going.
I Am Me!
I am the girl who came along,
    to turn your world upside down.

For better or for worse, is what we vowed.
    I am the girl who changed your life.

I stayed for better; you changed for the worse.
    I stayed near; you strayed far.

Your light went out; I lived in the dark.
    The heat went cold, the passion burnt out.

I am the girl who turned you around.
It always seemed so profound.

The lie we lived, our future denied.
The promises you made, on my weakness you preyed.

I am the girl who came along,
    to turn your world upside down.

You loved and lost; I loved and let go.
Time to move on, forward I go.

Untitled

Born into a place I don't belong,
Trying to fit into a space I can't stay for long,
With hopes and dreams I can't go wrong,
Standing on my own two feet, standing strong.

My past lined with so much regret,
The amount of faces I can't forget.
Looking for tomorrow to make me smile,
With the slightest chance that you will be mine.

I have a story to tell, it's a written passage,
Of how I came by a stolen message.
'Tis not mine but nonetheless I am the keeper.
For in the future I will possess, the hidden treasure from this quest.

Stumbled upon a day too soon,
I saw it all before my time,
My one chance to stay in line,
Not to fall off my path and fall behind.

Fitting in is such a task, especially looking through a mask.
Hiding the true potential when capable of a lot.

Behind A Smile!

Behind every face 'lies a truth.'

Day to day, face by face we encounter a smile.

Behind every smile tells a story.

Day in, day out hoping to find one to match mine.

Two sides to every story.

I'm left standing with half a book

Looking to complete the final pages to close the chapter.

Be Careful

She has everything you want but nothing of what you need, shortchanged and less of an insult to injury. Dreaming of forever, destined for failure.

The wise man said "if you stand for nothing, you fall for everything"

Your head's up high but your brain's down low. You run before you walk, talk before you think and regret before you've lived. Two people seemed right for each other yet wrong in all ways.

More than what meets the eye, not your typical girl. I came with but one instruction on my label: "handle with care". Give to receive, treat me how I deserve to be treated and live to be treated like a king.

All I want is someone to love me, WHOLE. Not a part time lover, not a momentarily love, not sometimes, some days but all the time. It will be a matter of time. Take the time to find me, take your time to know me because it will take time to love me. Don't love me today and forget me tomorrow, hold me today and always.

Sometimes it just hurts when you fall for someone who doesn't fall back. Left with a black hole. Something you wouldn't want to experience twice. So you hide away expecting "him" to find you.

Eyes

Angel Eyes is what I call him, beautiful hazel eyes, golden green that changes in the sunlight.

"Every time you see me what do you see?"

Sitting silently staring at me, an innocent dimple filled smile, curious to what you're thinking, guilty pleasures running through my head, heart racing, hands shaking.

I can still feel you as if his arms were warmly wrapped around me.
I can still taste you on the tip of my tongue as if his lips were against mine.
I can smell you as if we were cuddled up under the covers on a rainy winter's eve.
It's as if you're still here looking into my eyes but staring into my soul. Only you could see me for what's real and only I know the truth beneath your sweet lies, the why I smile each time.

You're afraid to take that next step you long to take but blinded by your greed of the lower mind you chose to think with. For the same reason I chose to forgive, for the same reason I let you back in, that same reason I stayed before, I'd the same reason deep down even if I do go I will still wait.

Convenient ey!

I'm not your best friend I'm your convenience.

She is far, I am here. I pass the time while you wait to hear…

Time goes by and your fakery multiplies. Listen to everything and Trust nothing you say.

You are my routine, nothing much more than a pawn to play so the days are less silent.

Don't assume you are……. your title "friend" has lost all meaning. Leaving the bitterness in my mouth to say you once were.

The time has past, the day has come, I bid you farewell with the set of the sun.

Dreaming!

Dreamland, where I live my best reality. Where I won't be penalised for doing all the crazy in my head.

Sensation tingling up my arms, creativity flowing through my body, temptation flooding my mind. Desire burning through my eyes, my body heating up, painting the town red, setting the world on fire.

Not a care in the universe, the angel on my shoulder is on vacation. No time to think, just enough time to do it all and reminisce later.

Stop me if you can! I dare you! Try!

Over thinking is overrated! Takes risk to chance a dare

Whom

Who do you turn to, to keep you warm,
who do you run to when it's all gone wrong.
Who do you call to put that smile back on,
who's there for you, even when on the other side of the world?

I am the friend you lean on, the shoulder you cry on.

I had that dream again, where I save you from it all, but when the morning comes, I wonder if I can handle the fall.

"Friend" is what I do best, it would hurt me if I tried to be any less.
To be more is what I wish to achieve.

Find Me!

The one part of me that's unreachable, it's buried below. I'm not allowed to tell you how to get there, your task is to get there.

I'm sitting here looking beyond the horizon, trying to see tomorrow. Covered with a thick grey, hiding its secrets.

Always on the right side of the wrong pillow. The tears that fall seem so pointless, never changing the facts.

Stuck in the wrong place at the right time to comfort my soul. I sit by myself wondering how soon.

It's all been said before, the music whispers it to me in the nighttime. It's all been written, even in the sky above.

The moon is full of secrets; it listens as I seek comfort. Many look up waiting for a sound but instead the stars twinkle for hope.

It will all come to part in time, lying here dreaming of when, but I wake, feeling I'm wanting for what's never coming.

The headache, burning tear filled eyes, breaking heart but yet a mask smile that covers up.

Drowning in Self pity is a pathetic look. Time to make change the facts. Leave the past, change the present and prepare for the future. Make it happen, bend the rules, find loopholes. Take chances, bet on a risk, I dare you!

To: Me, From: Me

He's sitting on my wavelength, blowing through my mind. His unbelievable talent filled creativity. The passion in his eyes with the love in his heart. Power at his fingertips, pen to paper or even written in the sky. A moment so short, made to last a lifetime.

In his own time but he's on the way.
Close by but not ready to show a face yet. For now I stay dreaming till he comes to wake me up.

Set out to find him and came across mirages. Wanting badly for it to be real and mistakenly settled. Feelings forged, the happiness was only an idea. Then the loneliness came flooding back after the lessons learned grime the chosen mistakes.

Time ticking by ever so slow, patience wearing thin. Quietly losing faith, silently crying. Eyes burning from the constant looking, soul screaming from the torture, mind deteriorating from over thinking and my body paralytic weary and tired.

Waiting in the dark, searching for the light. Thinking back, revisiting the past. Taking that trip down memory lane. Many wounds reopened, scars that opened my eyes. Lessons that now keep me on my toes. Warning signs I missed, stop signs I accelerated at. Foolishly rushed in, quickly disappearing into the quicksand. Drowning in my own sorrow.

I was thrown a rope by an angel in disguise, still too shy to reveal a face.

Waiting in the dark, searching for the light. Thinking now about my future. Bright as it may, is still far away.

Half on a maybe!
Completely drained, you were my drug, I was hooked. Little did I realise you were my poison, slowly killing me from the inside out. Left so fragile and frail, dampened spirit, torn heart.

Days I wished I could fly away but I was too weak to try. I would look up at the painting that was once me and smile, deep down terrified to look into the mirror to see what I've become, what I let you turn me into.

Too afraid to leave the dark and go into the light.

Dark grey clouds that covered my night blue sky. Heavy showers of rain came down, washing over me. Neither a shelter nor shade in sight as I walked along a lonely path that seemed never ending. Soaking from head to toe, shivering cold and scared stiff. The tears that followed got washed away.

Praying it all gets better soon.

Soon when the pain stops and the tests cease. Soon when the sun rises and a new day begins.
Soon when nothing bothers me.
Soon when it's all clear, the lessons from my journey.

In a world so bright yet we seem to live in the dark.

My back turned, one foot out the door and teary eyed. In my final wasted breath "what goes around, comes back around" with the door slammed shut behind me.

It's your turn to miss me. With the past picture bonfire alight, sipping on a sweet future filled glass of optimism.

Deleted images and blocked out memories. Changed locks and changed numbers. Reinventing me to differ from what was me, my mistakes.

Rewritten in the clouds after I rearrange the stars. Taking control of my future and learning from the past.

Sitting alone, waiting by the phone for a half decent apology.

Moving forward yet still holding back. Stuck between my four walls who saw it all, staring a judging.

Three words uttered "let it go". Like pulling a sword out of a stale wound, not easy to do and so painful.

Not a thought nor a whisper, not a squeak nor care as the time went by. Not a motion or approach. The silence that sheltered me and the music that drowned the thoughts out.

Up Against the Wind!

Silence......it filled the room and echoed through the walls. A dream of music and laughter to keep the smile.

Standing close to the edge, afraid to fall so I look beyond, across the water. So high up I can't look down. Carried by the ocean travelled by sea, finally here as I'm up against the wind.

Tired of staring at a reflection I don't recognise. Feeling weary, weak and fragile. With no one by my side to face it, I feel empty and misplaced.

Stuck! my feet won't move; they don't know which way to take me. The tears that fall lose meaning each time. I've lost the fight in me; I can't find any more reasons to. With a bruised spirit and tender heart I feel so lost. Time seems to pass me by without a second thought.

Hiding away from the world, in fear I can't face what it throws at me alone. Tired of having to do it all alone. Tired of searching for what may not even be there waiting for me. Tired of looking around at the others faces.

Who takes care of me while I take care everybody else?

Suddenly, my mind went blank, my lips were dry, the air was thin and the light went black. Silence echoed through my mind, body frozen stiff.

I'm not even sure how to feel. The truth has never hurt so bad. I have pity on myself, I can't even smile at my own reflection, I see the sorrow in my eyes. I feel the tears coming but I'm all cried out, nothing left but dust. Not even the music can cure this time. I feel hollow and empty. I can't even feel the beating of my own heart. I'm numb, I feel neither pain nor joy. Just a lifeless vessel left to float across life's ocean. I looked around, hoping for a sign, left with nothing.

Looking Glass

So beautiful and strong as the glass she looks through and as easily shattered by a force as agile as the swift wind. To dream big as the ocean but live carefree as the waves that wash the writings off the sand.

Leaving behind damages of a hurricane as her world is turned upside down. The grey clouds that darkened her night's sky, left in the dark alone, awaiting patiently for the storm to pass.

So beautiful as the glass she looks through. To him she was transparent but in the right light she would shine bright and full of colour.

Day in, day out. shadowed by the sun, night by night guided by the moon, watched over by her star.

Taken by surprise when hope came in the form of the most unexpected. But too afraid to try again, living in fear of another disaster.

Silence!

Silence makes you appreciate the music. The dark makes you appreciate the light. Sadness makes you appreciate the happy times. Yin and Yang, one can't live with out the other. Balance, to be equal, to have two halves make a whole.

I am missing the light in my dark. The music to break my silence. I sit looking above, questioning the clouds to give me a sign, to show me the moon, to light my path in the right direction. Walking this path alone, it feels cold and pretentious, having to fake a smile to mask the tears and cover the sorrow.

Adam had Eve, the animals went on the ark in twos; so why am I standing in one? Where's my balance? Yes I am my own whole and I am complete, but I should not have to walk alone. Everyone needs that someone else sometimes.

He reflects me, I see myself in him. This sparks my attraction maybe it makes me vain, but it also makes me certain.

K

> Don't make me pay for her
> mistakes and I shan't accuse you of
> his ways!

Such a simple matter, why do we make it complicated? The awkwardness between us, treading light to not cause upset. So determined to make it work.

I can't remember how this works, didn't remember there being so many rules in love. This isn't a game so why does it feel like I'm competing against the world?

So crowded, to many faces in the scene, not quite sure where I fit in. Stuck in a maze, not sure where to go. Just like a lost puzzle piece making the jigsaw incomplete.

Sitting in a daze, stuck in a trance. Always having just the right thing to say. Sometimes predictable, not sure what to believe anymore. I want to trust but with so many past tear-filled soggy pillows its hard to believe.

Giving me plenty a reason to doubt, I second guess my happiness. Wanting it so bad, still falling for it all.

Lying under the moonlight, the wind whispering to me, the sand hugging me, holding me close. The waves washing up reminding me of the truth.

Saying a little prayer, hoping for a sign, looking to the stars, to say its all mine.

Foreseeing better but expecting the worst. Promising the sun but only causing fires.

I want to know you for you,

to see what you hide behind that beautiful smile. Break the silence you keep, fill the air with noise. Open the door and let me in, I want to take a journey through your mind, I don't want to play guessing, I want you to tell me.

I don't want to fall in love with the fantasy but date the reality. I like the little things, the sweet thoughts that count. Late night cuddles with the early morning kiss on the forehead. The late-night goodnight call when you're away, just so yours is the last voice I hear. That sensual moment when we lay together, your hand gliding over my body whispering in my ear, exploring my mind.

The time spent together with each other rather than in each other. Simple pleasures that set me free. That I'm on your mind, that I'm not in this alone.

Don't talk, just act. Don't say, just show. Don't promise, just prove.

All In My Mind

So afraid to fail, afraid to disappoint, to not live up to expectation. Competing with an idea that lives in your head. How am I to know what I'm up against. Accept me for me and not what you want me to be.

Trying to feel comfortable like everything is ok when it's not and I'm constantly walking on eggshells.
Trying to keep the voices in my head, not blurting out too soon.

There's only so much one can do before it all becomes too much of an effort. Feeling like you're the only one trying, you might as well have been left alone. Nothing comes easy in this life but is anything worth this much effort and yet accomplished nothing. To keep trying seems foolish, but when it comes to the heart, it never quits.

The mind plays tricks on us and will take us in circles. Wishing, wanting and needing is a separate issue but all come from the same place but wanting something to be true and its reality may differ.

You cannot give a person their mind nor can you decipher for them; you can only hope for the best and what's meant to be will...

I'm exhausted to make something of a situation that is as if drawing blood from a stone. The male and female mind are very different but we're both human so we must feel the same at some point.

Too tired to keep up, mentally frustrated with this pointless process and useless exercise. It takes two.

Written

I've stopped writing, the paper doesn't feel the same as it used to. The inspiration comes from a dark place. It all sounds the same. Needed a change of tune, needed to smile.

The sound of those old piano plays in my head, still trapped in the past. Finding it hard to go forward. Wanting to escape the past; so, I'm frantic and running yet still not moving. I shouldn't rush happiness but afraid to be shadowed by the dark noise.

The pen feels cold, the paper rough. My fingers bleeding, feeling I've written it all. There's nothing more I can say. The silent times ahead force a new action.

Actions that are louder than words, time to break that silence. Nothing more said as I put my hands to work.

Going forth, the first step always being the hardest. Legs still a bit shaky, trying to stand my ground.
Not really sure how to go about it.

There is the light ahead, my reason to smile is right there. I jus have to cross this bridge alone.

Distracted

We let the littlest of things consume our concentration, then lose focus. The simple things we worry about, makes the biggest impact in our mood. Life is unpredictable; to try to focus on all the what ifs, we leave no time for living.

Trying to convince myself it's all senseless to stress over, yet it's all not that black and white anymore. All the shades of the rainbow in between cloud my judgement. I'm not sure what's left to do. Hope is fading, patience wearing thin, stress growing still I'm not comforted by the reassurance of others. Thinking they all just don't understand yet only trying to help.

One step at a time, taking it day by day, trying to drown out the noise. I'm missing something, trying to understand what, when it seems there's nothing more I could ask for. Thankful for what I have; yet still seems there's something I'm missing.

Found myself looking through the window again, stood silent in a daze. Mind running wild, reminiscing on the reasons, I smile. Soft silence echoed through the air as I watched the day pass by.

Wondering what was up ahead for me, whether it's worth the wait or should I let go now. Trying to be patient and think positive but what's in front of me scares me.

I'm not perfect, I come with a few cracks. Yes I have a past but I want to focus on the future, our future. I want to try this "something new" with you.

Memories Back Then

Wishing we never met won't change the facts, it won't rewind time, and it won't make me forget. Dreaming of a perfect tomorrow just makes me delusional. Being in denial only makes it hurt more. Praying even harder every night for the pain to stop, the memories to disappear yet I'm only forced to fall asleep and dream of you.

If only I knew then what I know now, I could have prevented the fall. I let the wall I built up crumble and fall at his feet only to be toyed with.

The silent days I enjoy best; yet the days filled with noise make me smile only to later cry. Stuck with this feeling I can't shake. It gets easier by sunrise to sunrise, but dawn reminds me of what I've left behind.

Easier said than done, moving on, a blissful thought with a harsh reality check. Left feeling like the punch line to a cruel joke.

My instincts were thrown off by his realism. Reading into what wasn't really there.

Stuck on the first page, staring blankly at the words. Trying to make sense of it all but confusing the matter even more. The pounding in my head matching the rhythm in my chest. Feeling lost yet out of control. Fate has left my hands, the ball no longer in my court. Seeing what I need and watching it stroll on by past me. The little things that throw me off focus, concentrating on the least. Trying to find my way back.

Starting from the beginning is the hardest, after finally picking myself up off the cold concrete, to walk my own path. Only to be thrown by an obstacle at every step. I don't want to lose you now; we've come this far. Reaching for a helping hand.

Drowning out the noise, filling it with the music, which makes me want to hold on. Speaking all the words I need to hear, the words I should say. Deep down I'm screaming out, yet the room is still silent with only the echoing of my tears as they hit the floor.

Disguised

Your first impression was false; you are nothing of what you appeared. You chased me until I chased back, led me to fall and watched me crash. Though not your intention yet you stood aside as I crumbled.

Pulled out before the damage was permanent, told myself it was for the best yet I could keep away. My thoughts haunt me daily; my dreams torture me with sweet lies of the impossible. Though they make me smile, within the flash of a second drives a pain to my chest.

Wanting it to be real, questioning why the universe won't let me be happy. Testing my faith, pressing my patience, wanting to give up yet a glimmer of hope still sparks.

I was born with the curse of wearing my heart on my sleeve not in my chest behind its cage to be protected. So, hopeful to find "him" and not have to search a long quest yet the waters look deep, and I can't swim. So afraid to keep trying and meeting the same failed results. So afraid it's all a lie, trusting no one.

Thought I had finally found something good but that was another lie. I'm tired, too tired to keep this up, just so tired to even try.

Lying here, silent and still gazing out the window looking for a sign. Looking to the moon to shed some light.

Like Shattered Glass

Like shattered glass, scattered across the floor.

The reality of it all started to sink in as I looked around the empty house. The echo filled the room and bounced off the walls. Denied my dream once more, my faith now torn into many pieces as I looked to the sky. Slowly drawing the curtains retiring to the bedroom, lying on the lonely sheets of memories torture.

Tears of a tired soul fall as I began to slumber.

Nothing lasts forever, the words echoed.

This was only the beginning and not the end. But the thought of starting over again seemed painful and pointless.

This is my story......who am I......you're about to find out.

www.ingramcontent.com/pod-product-compliance
Lightning Source LLC
Chambersburg PA
CBHW071221070526
44584CB00019B/3103